PLACE TO PLACE

RICHARD EYRE

To Lionel

with best wishes

Richard Eyre.

By the same author
Utopia and Other Places
National Service
Talking Theatre
What Do I Know?

with Nicholas Wright
Changing Stages

Adaptations
Hedda Gabler
Ghosts
Little Eyolf

to my granddaughters

Evie and Bea

in the hope that when they're grown up
something of me will remain with them

"Places themselves are made of words"

Charles Causley

The Smell of Places

It's the smell of places
I remember, the traces
of my grandfather, the waft
of pipe tobacco, the cuffed
oily tweed, furniture or floor polish,
horse shit, urine, Gentleman's Relish,
cider, over-ripe banana I didn't know
how to peel, a rich reeky near-guano.

Of course the smell from the swan's curl
of neck, the downy skin of baby girl,
my daughter's after her first bath,
talcum powder, her precious breath
blended with carpet, showroom-fresh,
aromatic as her delicious flesh,
and the bleachy fragrance of new paint,
our first house, our joint accomplishment.

The 'odour of sanctity' is not a whim,
it's the scent of rotting flowers that springs
from corpses of crazed saints who begin
fasting to remove the taint of sin.
It's the whiff of funeral parlours – acetone,
sweet-sour, hint of purifying brimstone.
The gas of cant's more difficult to ignore
but, like bigotry's fumes, mere metaphor.

A friend in Prague in '69
described her exocrine
reaction, a pungent piss-stained stink,
as Russian soldiers with a wink
pushed into her flat and her glands
protested as she raised her hands
and knew the 'smell of fear' was literal,
figures of speech ephemeral.

Dorset

"Fate is a good excuse for our own will."
     BYRON: DON JUAN

A photo of my father two years old –
A pea upon a pony, a rope a belt
To tie him to a saddle – told
Me that whatever fear he felt

He hid from his father, who would beat
Him with a riding crop for minor
Misdemeanours and would mistreat
His mother till my father cried, the whiner.

At thirteen in the navy – a cadet,
To whom the military discipline seemed
A blessing or at very least a debt
That did not need to be redeemed,

He – only, lonely – armoured like a wolf child
And less at ease with people than with horses,
Became a man who could only reconcile
Himself to riders and those who joined the forces.

To those with milder childhoods than his own –
Like mine for instance – his sympathies were strained:
Unhappiness was your fault. He was prone
To dismiss misery; it was a pain.

[3]

All despondency except his own
Was weakness, and depression he would think
A form of theatrics, self-indulgent, overblown,
Which anyway could be assuaged by drink –

Though "browsing and sluicing" was the phrase
In self-reflexive irony he'd use then follow
On to "hunting" and to "fucking" and in praise
Of both as much gin as you'd try to swallow.

"Enough is too little, too much is enough"
He'd chant, then "Time is short and we must seize"
(On what he'd call some bird or piece of fluff)
"Those pleasures found above the knees."

He did seize at every opportunity
Those pleasures and mostly was rebuffed,
And, if not, made it seem as if impunity
Was guaranteed and guilt stuffed

Into a corner where his conscience lay
Undisturbed by sense of duty to his wife,
By whom I mean my mother, who'd display
A bruised resilience in her daily life,

And answer his faithlessness in kind.
Shy, determined and attractive, "merry"
And by contagion with her husband, "unrefined",
Her friends would say and, after exile, solitary.

Exile, that is, from London where her heart
Remained until her mind's adventure
Into Alzheimer's and its brutal art
Led her to depression then dementia.

Their clocks were set in 1941,
It was the war that regulated
The times and places of their lives and spun
Their minds together while it separated

Their bodies, she in Windsor, Devon, Dover,
And he in Dunkirk and the Atlantic,
Until they came together to discover
In bursts of death-defying, frantic,

Acrobatic sex, what was the skein
Of thread that bound the ill-matched, child-like, pair
Together. I'm sure you think I should restrain
My prurience, but speculation's fair,

'Cause when they died I found a small brown suitcase,
Elastic-banded airmail-letters to the brim,
With USE OF H.M. FORCES printed on the face
Of blue notepaper. Anxious, I began to skim

The words my father never meant for me
And what I saw was quite enough to make me rue
The blunt invasion of their privacy
And wish I'd waved their intimacies adieu.

Their letters showed me that I'd been quite unjust
To judge their marriage by its failure,
When it started with such lavish, mutual lust,
So lovingly described with graphic genitalia.

I knew them only when the pulse of lust was stilled,
Replaced by rows that seemed to last a century,
And if his anger (or desire) was unfulfilled
There was somebody to take it out on: me.

I didn't say "Good evening, sir" – bad attitude –
To someone who he'd served with in the war.
He castigated me for being rude,
And shouted "little bastard!" though I was sure

That I was a changeling not a bastard.
If I had said so he'd have said "Don't be
Too funny" – but, little as I was, I'd mastered
Defences so that it was hard to wound me.

I was like Achilles, held up by my heel,
Dipped in the river of domestic strife,
Where, canny, I was learning to conceal
The bruises: closed, ironic, seared for life,

And timid, cautious, eager for affection –
But not too eager – uncertain, insecure,
While pining for conviction and direction
Meandering towards the adolescent lure

Of utopias, mirages to dissolve
The world's conundrums and to set us free –
Christ! Marx! Che! Mao! Marihuana! Sex! Absolve
The world of tiresome ambiguity!

At least I'd caught the knowledge germ
And knew enough of preservation to allow
Myself to teach my sullen self to learn –
A glimmer of a shadow of a shadow now.

The present charms the past by sluicing down
Whatever you have buried of the early years,
The half-remembered streets of childhood's town
And what you have exhumed is never clear.

A slurry of casual cruelties remains
To smudge the hint of half a father's love
And be replaced by neglect, indifference and pain,
As, sitting on his shoulders, high above

The high street, maybe five years old,
I swayed and swanked, the would-be lordly mahout,
My little hands in his, broad, hard and cold,
And ducked my head to lumber into shops and out.

So rare to find us partners, me on top,
That was what "grockles" and "electors" did,
Those ordinary people who liked to shop.
Not concealing his contempt, the objectors hid

From his all-embracing casual slurs –
"A matter of imbuggerance to me" he'd say,
And mean to brush them off like sticky burrs
So he could smile or smirk or sneer or bray:

"No, you FOOL, that isn't what I meant!
Much more offensive than a string of words,
If I'd meant to be insulting I'd have sent
A steaming pile of elephantine turds!"

(Which is what his father did at Bristol Zoo.
He masqueraded as his cousin on the Board
And ordered elephants to be delivered two by two
To his garden party. Laugh? He roared.)

I make him sound a monster when to be fair
You'd have been charmed as well as been appalled
By Snowey (for his lanky thin blond hair)
"You go too far" you'd say. He'd not be stalled,

You'd just have goaded him to speak
Of "arseholes", "jewboys", "niggers", "runts",
Scattered curses to provoke the weak,
"Fucking pricks" – you've guessed it – "fucking cunts",

And aimed at me it was: "Shakespeare's shit!"
Whenever I had provoked or irritated him
By showing off my unadmired success or wit,
But even so I never hated him.

When he died I sat beside his bed
And, foolish, thought at last that I was free.
I should have cried with grief. Or joy. Instead
I hoped for once that he would notice me.

Eggardon

*"It is only with the heart that one can see properly.
What is essential is invisible to the eye."*
SAINT-EXUPÉRY

Spiders of electric pylons trace
Their lines across the valley and
If you ignore their webs the place

Has barely changed since fences
Started to divide the land
Into bites for sale, the clearances

That made common grazing ground
Into owners' private plots –
Even the tumid Celtic burial mounds

And barrows, lynchets, standing stones,
Earthworks, ditches and chalk giants – the lots
Of Celtic legacies that no one owns

Or should, anymore than Norman churches,
Sandstone villages, hills and in between
The valleys, hornbeam, oak and birches.

It's a landscape that makes me now accuse
The dictionary of falsifying green.
It has its own spectrum, a myriad of hues

That as a child confused my heart
Because I only saw an opaque monochrome
And didn't understand the crucial part –

That my unhappiness was indivisible,
That I'd blindfolded myself at home,
That I'd made the essential become invisible.

Now, to flout the flat green undercoat
I see the tilted fields I once thought plain are dotted
With lustrous, iridescent colours that float

From an oriental paintbrush, flicked in tiny wedges
Then scraped and smeared and blotted
On thick viridian woods and hedges

That wrap butter-yellow rape fields pitched
In tint against flax-blue meadows infilled
With poppies, red, and opiate rich, it

Seems too good for God, it had to be a landscape man
That thought and modelled, sketched and willed
This into existence, a miraculously detailed plan

To sprinkle sheep on hills to make them speckle-
          white,
To cue a cantering fox to carve a russet furrow
To add an antlered stag to give a dash of ammonite.

A Bronze Age fort commands the countryside
Cocky as an Aztec temple on a plateau,
Beyond, the Blackdown Hills and the sea's wide

Glittering expanse that's rich with gems
Of sunlight scattered shamelessly
To seduce the eye and heart and to condemn

The poverty of my vision when I used
To come here, I thought then blamelessly
Bored, a teenager, who I would now accuse

Of being heartless, lazy if you will,
For not responding to what nature endows
Us with, like the absurdly happy trill

Of skylarks fluttering on air currents,
Buzzards above indifferent cows
Who munch and puzzle their deterrence

Of the universal flies who busk
And buzz above the freshly-minted cowpats,
Whose sweet scent mingles with the musk

Of cow-parsley and honey-suckle, sunflower-yellow
Dandelions and mustard tansy that
Jostle with mauve-topped clovers to become the
          fellow

Of lofty episcopal purple thistle-heads
Who nod grandly in the breeze and tower over
Elegant pale lilac scabious, well-bred

Edwardian ladies upstaged by a small chorus,
Of near-indigo white-eyed flowers called
Germander Speedwell and *Eye of the Child Jesus*,

Or *Hawk Your Mother's Eyes Out* where we lived. Bid
By me to know its meaning my father drawled
"It brings good luck" but I don't believe he thought it
   did.

THEATRE POEMS

The Start

The start of all rehearsals is the same.
Lines of curling silvery sticky tape frame
The set, and props and hats and skirts lie out,
Scattered ready for our childlike game.

In the ging-gang-goolie ring I call out my name,
Then my role's to propagate the common aim,
So, hopping heron-like, I talk about
The play, the plan, the shared terrain.

Virulent with nerves, I assert, indeed exclaim,
That we're like pilgrims, bonded by the claim
To labour for the mutual good and be devout
Believers in self-exposure without shame.

I'm faithless but for the faith which I proclaim:
That we depend on metaphor to sustain
The alchemy of the ordinary without
Snubbing our need to entertain.

I'm compelled to fan our fictive spark to flame,
And magnify our muted voice to shout:
There will be no failure and no blame!
The start of all rehearsals is the same.

Rehearsals

I like things to take the time they take
in rehearsal, I don't like to fake
the time it takes to unpack
a suitcase, sew a sleeve, crack
a nut or boil a kettle.

I like the way that people stutter,
interrupt themselves, utter
nonsense, hesitate and fail to find
the words and, longing for obscurity, blind
themselves to what they've said.

I like the garbled grammar, clumsiness, the want
of neatness and of order, the unconfident
rhythms of speech, mangled sub-clauses
and the silences, the unscheduled pauses —
silence till it hurts.

In rehearsal, the court of appeal
is life itself: how do we make our fiction real?
The jurisdiction only lasts until art's claim
that life lived can never be the same
as life observed.

It's true of all matter, that we're bound
by waves of gravity, light and sound,
plays and performers too. We can't inspect
the fictional event without an effect
on the object we observe.

[16]

Sometimes I think I've dodged the handicap
and cunningly managed to close the gap
between life and theatre, though if I acquiesce
to what has happily been judged success
that's what I regard as failure.

Tech

The actors stalk the set like awkward guests
Just put down at a themed costume ball;
Sniffing out their habitat, newly dressed,
Some say "We're play-acting, children after all,
It's not a life for grown ups" – grown up *men*
They mean. Women don't share their problem,
They are used to assessment and display,
Pretending in the constant gaze of males,
Small shift to do it for an audience who pay,
They're unembarrassed by something which entails
Giving birth, becoming physically engaged,
Even if only to a character on a stage.

In the theatre sitting in the semi-dark
Tired, febrile, end of tech day one,
My head an irritating question mark,
Nothing but what and why have I done
This production in this unwieldy way,
Why is nothing easy that was easy yesterday?
How do I achieve this maladroit scene change?
What can be done about the actor's wig?
Why does the familiar all seem so strange?
Why is the auditorium so big?

Why is the stage filled with unforgiving bulk
As unpoetic as a prison hulk?
In guilt and in despair I almost pray
That the whole preposterous enterprise will be
Burnt down that night. But only the next day,

Like the sun appearing unexpectedly,
All is well, the actors own the stage,
The play lives liberated from the page.

Opening

The show is over. The audience,
Merry, laughing, spent, spills
Into the street and restaurants
While the cell of critics go home
To perform their biopsies.
The empty auditorium still buzzes
With the orbit of charged particles
And motes of dust fall from the flies
Through the dusk to the bare stage.
In the corridors and dressing rooms
The actors, hot with triumph and requited love
Shower off sweat and make-up, loud in celebration.

A little numb and slightly pissed
I shuffle backstage, unable to match
The pitch of exhilaration, the hugs
Of gratitude, the tears of sharp relief.
I've been here before, I know the signs;
Wary of the aftermath, the judgements
And the silence, I can hear
The muttering of the trees
And the urgent need for approbation.

The End of the Run

We all say sloppy things, are not too bright,
but to me it always seems mysterious
that when actors meet the press they invite
mockery for being serious.

It's hard to talk about what it's like to act,
it's like breathing: what is there to say?
that you agonise and are wracked
in torment by acting in a play?

The job is this: pretend to artlessness somehow,
hold the mirror up to nature, simulate the real,
so why ask: how do you learn your lines?
or: who you are fucking now, please reveal?

They call actors *luvvies*, the self-christened *hacks*
who eschew adjectives like 'loyal' and 'gentle'
in favour of a kind of soporific anthrax –
patronising slurs like 'mawkish' or 'sentimental'.

Before those bitter cohorts have begun
their sneering litanies I recommend
they stop by the dock door when a run
of a triumphant play has reached its end

And watch the set dumped in a skip and trashed,
the costumes and the props sent to a store,
the metal, plaster, canvas, wood all smashed,
the thrilling suspension of disbelief no more.

A new show makes its claim on our emotions,
the past is past and our hard-nosed incentive
is, like gravity or Newton's Laws of Motion,
"We who live to please must please to live."

Rio: Musée des Beaux Sports

With apologies to W. H. Auden

About athletics they are always wrong,
The Commentators: how well they misunderstand
The sports competition: how it takes place
While someone else is eating or opening a window or
    just walking dully along;
How, when the audience is reverently yearning
For a miraculous event, there always must be
Others not especially interested, turning
To a spot at the edge of the track.
They never forget however
To make a painful failure run its course
Somehow in full close up or on the internet.
While the officials go on with their dreary lives the
    sportsmen are forced
To itemise their flops unhappily on TV.

In Bolt's 100 metres, for instance: how the high
    jumper turns away
Quite leisurely from the event; the long jumper may
Have heard the roars, the public overwrought,
But for him it was not an important success; the spots
    shone
As they had to on the black legs disappearing into the
    green
Outfield, and the ungainly shot putters that must have
    seen

Something amazing, a man running faster than
        thought,
Had something to compete for and carried calmly on.

FILM POEMS

The Dream of Film

CINEMA distributes the magician's gifts
of transforming scale and shape, shifts
size from creeping ants to arching monsters, lifts
threatening objects, landscapes which engulf you,
makes eyes the size of cars, hair into godly tresses,
defies thought and reason, compresses
time, expands it, translates the premise
of a quotidian world to a wizard's view.

SHADOW is the necessary part of light,
the grey stalker in films of black and white
whose dreams can sinuously unite
every day events and myth and fantasy,
making it possible to conceive
and catalyse fiction to stories we believe
can inspire and move us to deceive
ourselves into a wished-for ecstasy.

LIGHT works miracles, Fellini said;
in *La Strada* he spread a spectrum bled
of colour but made us see the circus red
as vivid, powerful and intense
as Hitchcock's *Vertigo* fluorescent green
which sacrificed the vocabulary of dream
for the colours of an emblematic scheme
where each hue held a literal significance.

FILM is a magic carpet which appears
to jump, negate and circumvent the barriers
of time and place to which reality adheres,
but for all the liberty of its conceit,
in theatre anywhere can be anywhere,
an empty stage a palace, a painted flat a square,
but anywhere in film has to be somewhere:
a street always has to be a street.

Development

You know, you have to speak our language:
Back end, territories and turnaround,
Hot actors, bankability and wattage,
Above/below the line, ballpark budget, falling pound,
The Industry, Academy and tax-credit scheme,
And you need input, you have to address
Our notes: the arc, the action, plot point, theme –
Write characters we can root for in the US!
A script doctor'll take your toney artefact,
Polish it until it's smart and funny,
And like a lot of projects that we've backed,
We'll package it with class though not with money,
'Cos frankly, even if your movie's almost ready,
It's too art-house, it won't play in Schenectady.

Day One

The location base: costume, make-up trucks and
                caravans,
Props and grips and camera, an HQ where plans
Pour forth to the invading army, which like real ones
Marches on its stomach, so sausages in hamburger
                buns
Are in demand: breakfast even though it's half past
                three,
Nightshoot ahead, daylight is our adversary.

It starts with handshakes, hugs perhaps. Did we?
Yes we did, a year or so ago or was it three?
Many faces seem familiar: Ben, Ben, Ronan, Peter,
Tristan, Karen, Daisy, Mike and Mike, Anita...
How are you? Fine, fine. What's this eh? You wrote it.
No, Shakespeare did. Oh yeah, Shakespeare? That's
                well fit.

What's the catering like? Fancy a fried-egg sandwich?
Is there a queue? I don't mind waiting. No, I'll get it,
                Rich,
You've got a long night. Ketchup? Yes, no, yes, HP?
I'm the outsider here, the crew all work regularly
Enduring long days or nights, up before dark, home
                after dark
Me? Once a year or less, to them directing is a lark.

Why are they staring at me, the ones I haven't worked
       with?
They're uneasy, sniffing, scrutinising me: is he calm or
       will he be abusive?
Like an orchestra waiting for the conductor's down
       beat
They're thinking: will this job be hell or will it be
       sweet?
They need me to make decisions, then the planets will
       align
And in a week's time we'll be dancing like a chorus
       line.

Let's do it, I say, put my polystyrene cup of tea aside
And point: let's start the scene here with the wide.
The DoP and I discuss the lens, the framing, shall we
       track?
The crew goes into action: camera, dolly, lights, the
       AD's talkback
Fizzes with instructions, props are ready, vehicles
       stand by, then
The actors come on set, rehearse, and we're in
       business once again.

Quiet please, the AD says. Turn over.
Mark it, says the focus puller. We're away.
Running, says sound. Speed, says camera.
There's a silence. And…Action, I say.

Location

Not quite a tourist – I am filming here –
I browse the Tower and its artefacts
With the swagger of an aristocratic voyeur.
The vitrines of sword and halberd, mace and axe,
Weapons and shining armour, burnish our
Inclination to embrace the syntax
Of vicarious violence, the acrid lure
Of brutality varnished by English Heritage text.

Here prisoner Raleigh translated Juvenal and Horace,
And the little princes studied irony,
"Lodged for safety" said their uncle, who taught
        Clarence
To snorkel in sweet white wine. Here Lady Jane Grey,
The nine day queen, leant how to dispense
With her head to avoid an awkward apostasy
Saying "Dispatch me quickly" so's not to give offence.

I marvel at the cunning of the torture tools,
Choke pears and thumbscrews, pillory and rack,
Considered and refined as if there were schools
To study giving pain. Women who showed "a lack
Of order with their tongues" had two large ferrules,
Iron semi-circles spiked front and back,
Around their necks to provoke agony and ridicule:
The "Collar of Torment" was its witty tag.

It's a commonplace to show disgust
At men's vileness, and titillation at the stories
Of consumption, evacuation, lust –
The kitchen, garderobe and bed-chamber glories –
That encourage us to feel they weren't like us,
And patronise their lack of flushing lavatories.
Do we feed our present national distrust
If we collude in condescending histories?

Historians have to tidy up the past,
Filter suffering with a rigorous sieve,
Leaving granules called the *Holocaust*
Or *World War One*, a causal logic, a narrative
That goes from then to then and then at last
Comforts us that there's no sacrifice left to give.
Our forefathers paid the price and in contrast
We can be spendthrifts with the lives we live.

The Controlling Part

*"The directing of a picture involves coming out of your
individual loneliness and taking a controlling part in
putting together a small world."*
        JOHN HUSTON

I'm the general of an occupying army
who'll bribe you to camouflage your house,
distress your immaculate facades,
do the same thing to your spouse.

I'll plant your streets with people
from another century, multiply them on the nod,
summon sun when nature's instinct fails,
make rain and snow, in short, play God.

I'll stand stock-still, observant
as a church-full of religious teachers
and unforgiving as a stalking hunter:
I'm shooting rare and vulnerable creatures.

I'll go as suddenly as I arrived,
leaving you dull smears of camera mark-ups,
the hieroglyphs and runes of red sticky tape,
and the white spoor of polystyrene cups.

Editing

It begins in fragments
no map but the script,
now superfluous, redundant.

What's on the screen
is the only evidence,
the sole topography.

On the page the words
CUT TO seemed enough
to get from here to there.

Transitions are the verbs of motion,
adverbs dictate the pacing:
slower, quicker, sharper, shorter.

Nouns supervise the process:
compression, distillation,
expansion, extraction, subtraction.

Scenes are re-ordered, pinched,
coiled, slabbed, sliced, cut away
like a sculptor's clay maquettes.

Adages breed: it doesn't earn
its place in the film
just because you've filmed it.

Junk your favourite shot,
the audience has no curiosity
about the hours it took to achieve.

The scene order's never the same
as it started; concede to
unsentimental objectivity.

The end can never be anticipated,
proof of the Four Quartets:
In my beginning is my end.

When you're finished, like Leonardo
looking at his painting in a mirror,
run the film at 10X speed

A sinuous line should run
from start to finish, no obstacles,
like a continuo held forever.

Screening

Five years since the idea was first
Discussed, then three years nursed
In development, barter, input, re-writes,
Costing, casting, scheduling, shooting,
Editing, mixing, grading, testing.
You have finished. A festival invites

You to stride the red carpet to a screening.
In an agony of ill-accustomed preening,
Flash photos, microphones, false modesty,
You shrink and hyperventilate
As the audience illuminate
Your film with their unaffected honesty.

They applaud, rising to their feet.
This is your summit, the job's complete,
It's downhill now and your hubris,
In vain isolation elaborated,
Fertilised and innocently curated,
Is punctured by an interviewers' chorus.

Q: "What drew you to the project?"
A: "Money, death and sex."
Q: "What was it like working with X?"
A: "Brilliant says it, not a thing to add."
Spinning the prayer wheel, you intercede –
Q (to self): "Do you feel that you've succeeded?"
A (to self): "I made the film. The reviews have not
        been bad."

Bridport

up the long incline to the railway station
cap, satchel, grey flannel shorts
two apples, one for to and one for fro
branch-line single-track Toller Powerstock Bridport
down the High Street to the Grove
third of a pint of milk, straw through tin foil
plasticine fly away peter fly away paul
chant by-the-shore-of-gitche-gumee
colour in Hiawatha's feathers
run banshee in ear-piercing spirals
forage conkers, beech nuts, pebbles
trudge back, cap skewed, tired legs
hand in my sister's hand
she seven, I five
unsupervised, home to home,
alone, a daily palindrome.

once waiting for the train
my half-chewed apple flew from my hand
rolled to the edge flopped on the track
as the train drew in I followed it
my sister grabbed my arm
yanked me like a coal sack
I fell yelling apple-less
to the comfort of the concrete
she wouldn't speak to me –
contempt or fear or something –
something like love perhaps.
60 years later while we ate lunch
by the bridge in Brantôme on the River Dronne

between the salade périgourdine
the confit de canard and the nougat glacé,
indignant in self-exile and self-righteousness,
she catalogued my cabinet of follies.
I didn't speak knowing that it was my turn
to pull her from the track on to the platform
but my hand reached out too late

the railway line is gone, my sister too,
the sharp tug of her arm long overdue

Stubbington House

The small black car shrinks
to a scar then a spot
and my mother is gone.

Small boys in grey shorts
turn away to hide
their pricking tears.

Gravel paths circle
late summer sunburnt grass
and an air of unconsidered cruelty.

At night under thin blankets,
my iron bed the aerial,
I have extra-terrestrial contact:

A crackling voice and a faint
stutter of music in the pink
earphone of my crystal set.

In the other ear I hear sobbing
in the high ceilinged room
and cawing of rooks in the tall elms.

Sherborne I

when I was fourteen
these nouns I prized:
breast, bra, skin and sheen
tongue, cleft, nipple, thighs

with addition of the adjective
female, curvy, naked, pubic,
or any gloss which could give
girls, sweet but not cherubic,

sexual promise in almost any shape,
with undo, unzip, unbutton, squeeze
bite, suck, stroke, lick, and even rape
the verbs which fuelled the fantasies

that thronged my adolescent brain
made me tumescent, drove my teenage
sexual longing, piqued my aching pain –
words consummated on a novel's page.

Sherborne II

I never knew I'd shared a room with Alan Turing –
A study, thirty years apart –
Until I saw its photo in a book exploring
The places and ideas of his heart.
He was the school's most dazzling mind,
In his or any other generation,
The Newton of computing, *wunderkind*!
Whose brilliance glitters still without my iteration.

They purged him from the list of the alumni
When he was criminally charged, defenestrated,
Found guilty of "gross indecency",
And, with his acquiescence, chemically castrated.
Time's alchemy turns shame to glory,
Erodes base defamation, glosses calumny:
Outside our study a plaque now tells his story,
And, though I was expelled, they write to me for
    money.

In and Out

At Dunkirk he commanded the last boat
And mostly spent his naval career afloat,
South-East Asia with a destroyer fleet,
Then the tedium of Portland had him beat.

The navy wouldn't let him go to sea
So my father left at 43,
Became a farmer, the real thing,
Wheat and cattle to begin.

He went at lunchtime to the local pub
Though still retained his London club;
He drank pink gin there, in the country stout:
The White Horse and the *In and Out*.

In the pub he'd heat a poker
And plunge it (something of a joker)
In his Guinness: "A life restorer!"
In his gin he'd drop angostura.

He wanted me to join but was frustrated,
Because the club – I now confess – I hated.
There I always was as ill at ease
As a Hutu in a crowd of Tutsis.

He'd parade my wife like an Angus steer
In the pub, hinting with a leer,
I was lucky to get such a prize for free.
In his club he'd do the same to me.

"This is my son" said the veteran of Dunkirk.
The Brigadier asked me what I did for work,
I told him. "Theatre eh? Must be a lot of sex.
Here we hide our women in the annexe."

"He means fucking in the club's guestrooms,"
Interpreted my father. "That's why," booms
The Brigadier, "We call it here the In and Out!
Just make sure you don't get 'em up the spout!"

Saigon

In the summer of sixty-six
An almost gap-year tourist,
In Saigon City I stayed three days
In an unofficial naïve haze.

Like other almost-innocents,
I'd heard of active war and sensed
Through my unformed sceptic prism
That "military advisors" was a euphemism.

I saw Saigon airport was a rookery,
Starfighters nesting in the aviary
Of a parliament of B Fifty-Twos,
Coddled by their service crews.

The town, once brightly butterflied,
Was mottled, poisoned, khakified:
Through willowy rainbow silk cheongsams
Stalking wolves crept among spring lambs.

The still-French cafés I remember,
And the scent of mint and coriander,
The reek of *Old Spice* and *Lucky Strikes,*
The mopeds' horns, the swarm of bikes.

I met a US soldier in a bar,
"It's my job," he said, "making war";
Asked if he felt the North should still exist,
"It's their fault," he said, "being communist".

At home my new-found indignation
Was premature, Vietnam was an operation
Too remote to interrupt a London life,
While Cambodia was waiting for the knife.

I went to Angkor, I was then in Eden,
Not a glimmer that the war was leading,
In the summer of nineteen-seventy,
To the gifts of Nixon's plenty.

Before Pol Pot, before the murderous abyss,
I had once thought: Paradise, it is this.
Now I think, in year two-oh-one-seven,
If war is hell, where on earth is heaven?

Edinburgh

It must have been late December.
I know because, with cat-like grin,
You said we were first-footing
As we lay in bed, sprat-sprawled,
Dizzy with discovery.
I was your cartographer,
Charting the landscape of your face,
The shallow valley of your throat,
The perfect tumuli of your breasts,
The travertine plateau of your stomach,
The downland between your thighs,
The long lanes of legs, the alleys of the toes,
My fingers drifting from a continent
Of flesh to an archipelago of touch.
I know the map's co-ordinates now,
How to read your legend,
The direction of your compass rose,
How to render you in three dimensions.
I had no idea the scale
Would translate map to life
For 47 years.

Nottingham

When I was thirty I was stalked
By abstract nouns whose shadows
Swayed behind me as I walked
Beside the would-be desperadoes

Who sang of Revolution, Hope
And Freedom, Progress, Strife,
All well beyond the scope
Of what I knew of life,

Made up for by my friends' grasp
Of "praxis" and of "hegemony",
Of capitalism's "final gasp",
Of Trotsky, Marx and Gramsci,

Whose prosecutor aired these fears
In court: "We need to stop this brain
From functioning for twenty years";
Prison's loss was death's vain gain.

But Gramsci's prosecution's heirs can claim
The *Daily Mail* to air their grudges
And, without a trace of shame, name
Those enemies of the people – judges,

Who did nothing but declare
The law, and that history only swops
When it serves us up its fare
In different dishes, same grey slop.

Though none of us anticipated
That the world would be for sale,
That to be poor would be to be hated,
That all ideals were born to fail,

That socialism would become
An almost religion almost dead,
That faith would multiply its young
And intolerance become its daily bread.

That politicians would transmute
To invertebrates governed by PR,
That a malign buffoonish brute
Would be the world's chief puppeteer.

That binary digits would evangelise
For universal equality and spawn
A parasitic cell which magnifies
To form a continent of porn.

That oceans would swell when icebergs unseal
And forests burn; that fossil fuels would blot
The whole earth's body and congeal
In giant fungal melanoma spots.

Were we gullible or naïve?
Or innocently guilty to hide
What we chose to disbelieve –
The human race's urge to suicide.

We didn't see, when we said that we must
Have change, that those who disagreed
With being fair and being just
Were living by a different creed.

When my father said that striking
Miners should be shot, why did I
Think it was a joke, disliking
It but not disputing? And why

When there are no more miners
Left to shoot do I listen
When society's blind designers
Tell me all that's lead still glistens?

And is there no archipelago,
No little islands of dissent,
To free the mainland and say "no"
To all the Right's vast regiment?

If it's not enough to love
One another or to die and blame
Ourselves, like Auden, then remove
Our young opinions in a waste of shame,

What *should* we do as we trump,
Mute and leaden-footed, towards
The vile and noisome future slump?
Is it impossible to speak the words

Where are the snows of yesteryear?
And answer:

They're here,
They're here,
They're here.

Budapest

Only the Boots! the guidebook says,
Of a statue of Stalin that was scythed
At the knees in Budapest during the days
That the Revolution thrived.

Here colossal gnomes are gathered,
In a barren garden called Memento Park,
Icons of Soviet worship, well-weathered
Effigies of Lenin, Engels, Marx,

Who point index fingers like traffic cops
Towards Freedom, Progress, New Tomorrows,
For men with thighs as wide as rooftops,
A chorus line of flag-waving heroes.

A severed head of Stalin, daubed with paint,
Has been scrubbed by State Security,
Trying to expunge the enduring taint
Of spilt blood ordered by committee.

In the Bucharest revolt a thousand died,
I saw their virtual shadows where they lay.
Flowers and cards and candles still described
Their bodies, like Hiroshima's ghostly underlay.

Securitate dumped the workers numbed by cold,
Who fell from Ceauçescu's palace floors,
No lack of labour but never enough gold
For all the taps and handles on the doors.

In the gift shop at Memento Park
They sell Party songs and Soviet pins,
Giggling keepsakes stamped with satire's hallmark:
The Last Air of Communism in paint-pot tins.

Articles of Faith

*"Man cannot make a worm, yet he will make
gods by the dozen."*
          MONTAIGNE

I cannot stand the brutish spite,
The toxic absolutes of wrong and right,
And all religions' seeming need
To fertilise division then to breed.

I cannot stand the bland conceit,
The smugness and the self-deceit,
The feeble blistered fairy stories,
The tedious inventories,

The litanies and maudlin
Chants of punishment and of sin,
The sick devotional refrain
Of guilt and suffering and of pain,

The obligation to placate
The almighty, the casual hate
Of those who do not share
Your chosen mode of daily prayer,

Who bow when they should kneel,
Face east to express their zeal,
Bang their heads upon the floor,
Flail their backs to create gore.

I don't care whether on your cross
Or torture stake a deity was lost,
It's an act of hubris to say he died
To save the world and one I can't abide.

Nor the pitiable confusion
Of those who're mired in self-delusion,
Hovering above death's plimsoll line
Waving a passport to a life divine.

Immortality does not seduce –
Eurydice was not rescued by Orpheus,
And resurrection can't convince –
The frog was not transformed into a prince.

Each religion offers to transcend
The inevitable all-consuming end,
And peddles – what? Consoling pity,
i.e. death ushers in a life less shitty.

Jehovah, Yahweh, Odin in Valhalla,
Christ, Krishna, Zeus, Quetzalcoatl, Allah
Compete to be the great I AM,
Porous and insubstantial as a hologram.

The return on loyalty is a hereafter –
Elysia, fields of innocence and laughter,
A New Jerusalem, a House of Song,
Nirvana, Heaven – they're all wrong!

Why would you think to slaughter
Young girls – same age as your daughter –
For a prophet's pledge that you can exercise
Your right to virgins in the Paradise?

All faiths and all religions are extreme,
Reason suffocated in an opiate dream.
They will not make you content or sure,
They are there to teach you to endure.

Why should we give the name of god (small case)
To what we cannot fathom or can't face –
Like space, or nature, or how we came to be
And why. Why can we not just call it mystery?

And if there's any saving to be done
From trespass and transgression, trust the one
Who can give you absolution and proclaim
That empathy and faith are not the same:

Look in the mirror, you'll know who to blame.

Manchester

Next to the photo of his sister,
Year Six, there's a small black flag
Pinned to his wall, between the class list
And the timetable. He can't make out the tag

In curled white writing. Arabic, he thinks.
He knows that there is no god but god,
And finds that the tautology suits him:
No one ever calls a true believer odd.

He sits on the bed, like a fisherman
Mending a net, his knees spread
Wide, between them a backpack, soft
But heavy, heavy as a head.

Try it on, said Amir, fitting it
Over the shoulders, closing the clasp,
Coiling the wire. Fits nice, he said,
Don't snatch the handle, only grasp.

No fear now, he knows happiness will seek
Him like a lover, his radiant hate
Carbonised, compressed and clear,
Will carry him, a diamond, to his fate.

He won't hear again his mother in the kitchen
Listing his shortcomings since his birth,
Or the cries of those infidel children
From Winstanley to Saddleworth.

Out of my Mind

The irksome legislator in my head
Is there to rule on things unsaid,
Not called to arbitrate or decide
Whether it's appropriate to divide
The brain and mind and which one
Controls the other: which the sun
And which the moon? Is the plan
That man makes his fate or fate the man?

He appoints the grimy babushka
Who sits sourly at the corridor's far
End and monitors the thoughts unbidden
Which offer lust and greed and envy, hidden
Feelings which come as covert visitors,
Cloaked and hooded, eager inquisitors
Who catechize, apply the polygraph,
And secure answers from my other half.

I have idle guards failing to protect
Me while I sleep, neglecting to deflect
The spiders and guerrillas of my dreams.
They leave my arching doubts and silent screams
To be handled by the stern police of reason,
Or the unctuous priest who threatens treason
To my cause by hints of moral duties, oughts
That nag and flicker at my thoughts.

None of them bothers to evict the ghouls
Which lodge in my consciousness (or soul?) –
The inner Thatcher, Lothario, or Christ –

Or stem the urge to kow-tow to the zeitgeist
Or close the traps that melancholy brings
That spit forth darkness, serpents, wolves, wild
        things,
That have to be placated, helped to pile up sand
Against anxiety, to change 'anguished' into 'bland'.

I defy the dejected bitterness of age
That even medication can't assuage,
In present happiness I can't disprove
The blessed, improbable, reality of love.

Brook Green

From my top floor window I can see,
through the refracting urban prism
of roofs and aerials, chimneys, trees,
the shark's-jaw arch of Wembley stadium.

A vicarious competitor, I can snoop
on a half-naked man gross as 40 watermelons
bending belly-first towards his coop
to release his treasured racing pigeons.

The babble at the French school is my siren:
FIVE TO NINE! The mothers give high-pitched
greetings to their friends, drop their children
with the promise that they'll be fetched,

As they are at precisely half past three,
after they've trotted hand in hand –
not being English, boys and boys in harmony,
girls together, girls and boys unplanned.

Most days a supermarket van's beeping whistle
signals deliveries for a neighbour's larder,
plus Persil, Andrex, Pledge and Mr Muscle,
the sacred pantheon of domestic order.

On my desk I have a leather calendar,
a tattered relic but still whole,
from Scott's first expedition, pathfinders
for the race to the Antarctic pole.

It was my grandfather's. Inscribed in a
faint gold-leaf on the back – *Discovery*
this was her charter Rule Britannia
24th July 1901 – Empire's jubilee.

My grandfather returned, became a father,
the pigeons returned to their loft,
the child returned to its mother,
the crates were emptied, the van drove off.

In my eyeline too I have atop a tripod
a little head, in crystal glass that sparkles,
of Ganesh, the elephant-headed Hindu god,
the God of Writing and Removing Obstacles.

I know one day a GANESH van will deposit,
armed with exculpating camcorders,
four policeman outside the house opposite
who'll be following Home Office orders.

They'll emerge swiftly with men who can't go back
to any country they might call their own,
and they'll bundle them like refuse sacks
into the van, fate and destination unknown.

The black people: they'll say there are too many
the brown people: they'll say there are too many
the Jews: they'll say there are too many
the Arabs: they'll say there are too many.

Then they'll knock on my door: Are you well?
Seen any trouble, aggro? *Acrimony?*
No, I'll say, Nothing, nothing unusual.
The cowards, I'll think, there are too many.

Chichester

Seagulls yap and the sighing rasp
Of circular saw joins the woody click
Of crown bowls: this the soundtrack.

A leaf falls like a wounded parachutist,
A mobility scooter hums along the pavement
Like a lawn mower: this the action.

The Romans built walls around the city;
We build car parks. Is the aim the same?
Who are we keeping out? The young.

Passport control stops everyone
Without grey hair. The curfew falls at five.
The Georgian red-brick shops close up.

Eighteenth century silence,
But for an accordionist traducing
The definition of a gentleman.

Here the old hold hands,
And I forget I'm one of them
Pretending to be immune to time.

Then *wehhaaaay* the barbarians arrive!
Heads crowned with feathered fascinators,
Ripe bodies sheathed like evening gloves

On pig-plump arms, barefoot, high-heels
In hand, like buckets at the seaside,
The women totter, sway and shout

At their blue-black-suited-brown-shoed
Ribbon-tied-at-half-mast men,
Giddy with drink and wages squandered:

"You arsehole, I knew it was a dog!"
Here is the town's body less observed,
The blood that fills its arteries,

Revealed through the Teresa Rizzi rosé
Magners cider, Ruddles, Purple Rain and Cheeky
        Musk,
As the day at Goodwood Races turns to dusk.

The Tower

This is the story of a burning tower
That spun from flame to furnace in an hour.
Seventy-two living bodies were cremated,
A barnacled charnel-house created.

This is the flotsam of a tide of grief,
Soaked notes, dear Mum, dear Dad, that lie beneath
Cling-filmed froth of flowers, furry toys and dolls,
The insignia of mourning protocols.

These are the scavengers, little TV gods
Who spread their tentacles, one-eyed cephalopods,
And feed on wounds a sea of tears won't heal,
Baying: "Tell me, tell me, what do you feel?"

Anger, say those whose homes have turned to ash,
An oceanic rage that's poised to crash
And drown a childless mother stammering in vain:
"I can only say, how can a heart let in so much pain?"

The Mark on the Wall

"One cannot think well, love well, sleep well, if one has not dined well."

VIRGINIA WOOLF

I didn't know, said Nellie Boxall,
While I raked the ash and blacked the grate
Laid the fires and brushed the floors,
Shopped and cooked and scoured the pans,
Waited at table and polished the silver,
Emptied her chamber pot and washed her smalls,
That I was a mongrel,

That I had a commonplace mind, an inferior nature,
Was crude and coarse, smelly, sweaty, unrefined,
An indelicate soul and an expendable one:
I heard her say of Lottie Hope during an air raid
"That poor gaping imbecile my charwoman,
What an irony if she should escape
And we be killed."

She called us the "saarvants", Mrs Woolf,
Said that we were blabbermouths,
The more you talk, she said, the less
You have to say. "One," she said, "has never
Stood at a wash-tub". Why not? Why was it me
Not her? I'd have liked a maid of my own,
A room would have been nice too.

Why couldn't she expend a little
Dribble of imagination, defy
Her need for self-concern
And care for me, a servant,
Not because I was poor or born unlucky
But because I was human. Or does that
Take a special genius?

"If you do not tell the truth about yourself,"
She said, "you cannot tell it about other people."
She didn't lie about what she didn't know
Of our lives – the "lives of the obscure"
She called them – although she did know
How to summon "waaards" and make them
Dance like they were weightless.

The chronic English illness, she once said,
Was hypocrisy, so I'd have valued,
Before I was employed by the actor
Mr Laughton and she had no domestic staff,
Her revelation, like Archimedes in his bath,
That always having had a servant it did hurt
To find "the horror of" – oh my lord – "the dirt".

Lampedusa

Virginia Woolf was a snob
Larkin was a misanthropic wanker
Lawrence was a fascist fucker
And Eliot didn't care for Jews.
They didn't have the luck
To be alive and writing now
And see that our compassion
Trumps their genius.
They didn't have the privilege
Of living when the Middle Ages
Have been so thoughtfully revived
And religious wars, crusades
And public executions flourish,
While famine, poverty, ignorance
And neglect caper Bosch-like
While the city in the background burns.
The word 'community' is invoked
As the public poultice for concern
And we piously delude ourselves
That our caring speech and love-willed
Protestations can placate
Psychosis, fanaticism and hard hearts.

6 infants, 2 babies, 4 lifejackets
3 women and 1 man – who has their passports
And their cash – are on a half-inflated,

[68]

Fragile, rubber boat, frightened,
Cold, hungry, sleepless, grieving
For their husbands drowned
In the Mediterranean night.
Does my compassion help them?

Box

"A bay tree tells you the state of your marriage:
if it flourishes so will you."
        COMMON SAYING

nature's an experiment in seeing
to be explored and a garden
is a laboratory for measuring
your life in seasons

each leaf, each stem, each plant
swells, shrinks, discards
what it no longer needs –
a world entire, the thing itself

a choisya started as a cutting
would now dwarf an elephant
and once-tiny tendrils of wisteria
have stems like muscled forearms

a bay tree shrub, a marriage-gift,
looms higher than a horse
a passion-flower born in a beaker
disperses like a benign pandemic

bluebells, wild orchids, aquilegia,
daisies, primroses, anemones,
hop clover, cowslips and buttercups
appear gladly, uninvited
we've signed a little patch of earth

with our own hands, the same that reach
across the sheets at night
for company

Minchinhampton Common

walking at midnight in the day's t-shirt,
up the thin lane above the valley, half-drunk,
a tree in silhouette shows me its neat skirt
clipped by the gently puffing sphinxes
who lie dozing round its trunk.

in the slate-grey-less-than-quarter-light
the continent of tufted grassland is deep viridian,
while the vast cobalt-violet sky's still bright,
outlining a horizon with a steady hand
to bisect the soon-be-indigo night from day.

dabs of flaming sodium street-lamps glow
like torches lit to drive out spirits
from the necklaces of terraces below
or scare the dragons which poison wells
when the sun turns to the south.

I slip on a crusted cowpat, lie back,
laugh, and look at heaven's blink –
stars, galaxies, nebulae – while the insomniac
cows snort at me for daring to imagine
we're the only ones with life.

Box in Winter

Winter sun is iced on ground glass;
It coats the blades of grasses,
Blesses the anemone pearls,
Graces the rosehip gemstones.

Leaves have lost their loyalty,
Blown away, dropped out;
Earth, their refuge, draws in its breath
And the seeds beneath await their call.

Something is in the air, invisible,
An almost breeze: almost motionless.
The orchestra of branches is poised,
Waiting for spring's downbeat.

Mystery of Things

"What is the cause of thunder?"
                KING LEAR

Evie, age 7½, tells me that thunder
Is caused by rain gathering under
Colliding clouds which creates a flash
When the individual raindrops smash
Into each other and a sound is made
By the explosion like a giant grenade.
I start to say – with a degree of tact –
That I don't think it's scientific fact,
When Bea, age 4, asks me what leaves are for.
The sisters are much too clever to ignore
And if I were as smart as them I would
Admit we're never wiser than in childhood.
I start to explain "photosynthesis"
And stumble in avoiding "hypothesis",
"Hydrolysis" or any temporising Greek –
In bullshit I'm an expert, in botany weak,
Like many practiced bluffers I think once
That I have named a thing it'll be an affront
To reason to question further: what do leaves *do*?
Reluctant to explain I start anew
When Evie interrupts me, says a tree breathes
Through the surface of its leaves and receives
Its food from air, its energy from light,
Leaves are its clothes, they keep it warm at night.
Which will do for me, even if I'm near
To saying to these girls most loved, most dear,

That nothing has a point in nature, that's
Its point, things just are – with two caveats:
Remember when you give each thing a name,
That to label and to grasp is not the same.
To catalogue the work of nature brings
A vocabulary to the mystery of things
But learn the tradecraft of god's spies,
Turn up each leaf: knowledge is the prize.

Sycamore

Here is a sycamore leaf,
whose five-lobed leaves
curl as it floats to ground
like an upturned umbrella,
red stem flowing into
green-blooded veins,
outshone by mothy
marbled seed pods,
whose whirling rotor blades
emerge from limey
frogs' scrotum sacs,
spin and land reluctantly
on the umber earth.

The young trunk is dark
skin-smooth, pink-grey;
age will crack its bark
into lizards' scales
on wind-bleached, hairless
arms which will beckon,
waving craggily
to the coming rain
and shrug goodbye
with thin-twigged fingers
to the departing sun.

The fig-like fruits, small furry balls,
have been harvested since
the not-prophet Amos

said: "I was no prophet,
Nor was I a son of a prophet,
But I was a sheep breeder
And a tender of sycamore fruit."

Perhaps he knew how to praise
trees that give birth
to leaves and fruits,
or who to congratulate
on their invention,
their preposterous ingenuity
and their careless alchemy.

Seeing nature, said Constable,
is an art like any other,
a skill as hard and admirable
as reading Egyptian hieroglyphs.

Passion Flower

There is a vine of passion flowers
That grows outside our kitchen door.
The modest green pods form like chrysalises
Then disclose their riches in a show
That butterflies must envy for their feckless
Intricacy and their lush extravagance.

I want to ask the flower:
Why? Why do you bother?
Don't you know a single yellow
Buttercup a thumbnail's width across
Enchants, while fields of them capsize
Our hearts and overwhelm our eyes?

Spare yourself the effort

Of painting filaments white and purple
Of twining brown curls into plaits
Of making fairground waltzers
Of hammer-like soft anthers
Of sculpting small testicles on stigmas
Of blackening furry fairy circles
Of drizzling them with red pustules
Of showing off, of self-display,
Of drawing the attention of Conquistadores

To the true apostles in your ten white petals
To the crown of thorns in your corolla
To the spots of blood that inscribe its hub

To the tendrils' lashing whips
To the stem's scourging pillar
To the five wounds of your stamens
To the three nails of your pistil stigmas
To the spears of leaves
To the white of purity
To the blue of heaven
To the purple of sanctity
To the holy grail of the ovary
To the fruit which is the Earth
To the salvation which is the promise

That the Saviour has not fulfilled as yet.

For the greater glory of that conquering Lord
The Spaniards swallowed up your native meanings:
Tonantzin the Aztec mother-goddess
Became the Virgin of Guadeloupe,
And the Mayan Sun-King Kinich Ahau,
Who grasped your unchristened splendour
When it sprouted from a human head
And sacrificed his own to the obsidian knife
To be resurrected in crops of maize and vines,
Was absorbed into the Passion of the Christ
Who rose up as the new spring greened.
Utilitarians can claim your herbal usefulness,
Or atheists like me your decorative glory,
But in Japan, where the Passion Flower
Grows unburdened by our Christian iconography,
You're as Hyacinthus to the god Apollo,
Wilde's green carnation to the feast of panthers,

A gaudy gay advertisement for sexual proclivity
By a flower which is, appropriately, double-sexed
And is an image that could be painted
By Georgia O'Keeffe. Of an arsehole.

For Tony at 80

Forgive me, Tony, if I celebrate
your birthday in a form you've made your own
and in the same metre try to imitate
what is your literary flesh and bone.

I know that imitation's flattery's mate —
priestly genuflections and flunkeys' bows
are society's icing, which of course you hate:
you want as much truth as humankind allows.

I first met you in the early 80s
in the NT's green room, when I was loath
to leave that life-devouring Thespian Hades
where it helped to be a man, or drunk, or both.

You wore your uniform of denim, faded
like a mechanic's, a French railwayman;
you smiled, red wine in hand, as you dissuaded
your burly crew, who revered you as a shaman,

From thumping some milksop twat who'd not
appreciated Glover, Rutter, Shepherd, Hill,
or objected to their Yorkshire scattershot
"less noise, more sense," you said, until

The crowd subsided and I shook your hand.
"I've read your work," I said and tried to quote
a line from *August 45,* full of loss and
pain, and you said "That's not quite what I wrote,

It was '*smoulder*' not '*burn for*' in my sonnet."
humbled but too insecure to show it
then I began my exegesis on it:
the life and works of Harrison the poet.

I learned your raw material's stuffed like evidence
in quarto notebooks of quotes and chance remarks
and fragments culled and beaten into sense
and your several rooms in Gosforth Park.

Where, after oysters you had shucked,
you gave me sea-bass cooked in salt and rosemary,
new potatoes, samphire salad, and then we tucked
into cheese, with jelly from your medlar tree,

And I discovered that gewürztraminer
is not an Alsace region but a grape,
and that behind your often grave demeanour
a mordant wit would frequently escape.

I found that, like a sculptor, your work was hewed,
carved out of stubborn blocks of words –
Latin, Greek, Italian, Hausa, Czech, construed
into eloquence from – well, you'd say it – turds.

"The beat is in the blood," you wrote, encrypted
in our veins and should be pulsing without waiver,
while the whole body should be conscripted
with mind and ears and lips and tongue to savour

Language, to make it dance from East to West.
and in New York, London, Delphi, your work succeeds
in a universal bardic conquest
for you, the baker's son from Leeds.

You're tender, stoic, tough and taciturn,
often stubborn, not beholden, free
to bollock, blast and castigate and burn
your enemies – without recourse to allegory.

I've known you now for 30 years or more
read all your poems, films and plays,
I've a superfluity to thank you for,
yet from all your work two items still amaze

And startle me. Some literary fellows,
professors, masters of the intellect,
confront their opposites who, with atavistic bellows,
burst out of crates with pricks erect –

The *Oxyrhynchus* Yorkshire satyrs.
They wave their cocks and stamp their clogs
and in demotic language settle matters
with the reigning cultural demagogues.

[83]

Fierce, passionate and magnificently gross,
in *Trackers* you gave us a paradigm
of how to be ourselves, yet make us close
to lives two thousand years ago in time.

You seduced us into managing the jump
between the past and present, High and Low –
Sophocles and Harrison combined to dump
our notions of a well-made theatre show.

And in case Sophocles might complain
that you'd usurped his play and made it up,
you drank his health each night in *brut* champagne
from a three-thousand-year-old Attic cup.

But of all your works that speak to me,
that touch my heart and atheistic soul,
not one speaks so vividly as *v.*
none has such power to inspire and to console.

V.'s the syntax of my daily life
the valences of soul and body, heart and brain,
of family, freedom, culture, husband, wife –
the opposites that my heart contains.

You roam throughout this territorial divide
for harmony and often find despair
which, though not your constant state, is allied
To sadness or to worse and I'm aware,

[84]

Because you told me once, that you'd go mad
if you couldn't write, that writing is a kind
of antidote to bedlam, giving the bad
thoughts and feelings form to purge the mind.

Reticence is the usual English mode
and RP – like my voice – is the default tone,
which *v.*'s direct address sought to erode
and the tyranny of "good form" dethrone.

You articulate a sense of place and class
between your heart's demand and your head's call
and always try to pierce the ceiling's glass
to make art accessible to all.

But, like Chekhov, you say "Don't offer pap,
bring the people up to the level of the art,
don't dumb it down, don't serve them crap,
don't patronise, speak simply from the heart."

When I became director of the NT,
I asked what I should choose to do, what play.
"Improve the wine," you said; it was not to be.
and of my verses now you'd surely say:

"Don't give up the day job, show concern
for language, rhyme and rhythm, look with open eyes
at everything around you – oh and spurn
those British Empire honours I despise."

You offer tough love and so my bequest
to you should be an enduring Eyreloom
that's suited for such men, as Yeats suggests,
who come open-eyed and laughing to the tomb.

So, no, I haven't baked a birthday cake,
or served champagne in a cup from ancient Greece;
instead I have a gift from William Blake —
a yearning prayer for Love. And Mercy. Pity. Peace.

The Dodo

Apparently the dodo didn't only die
By human hand and misdemeanour;
A twist of evolution was the alibi,
As with the Polaroid and the Ford Cortina.

Nature's unforgiving, so is commerce;
The former hosts the kind of germ that brings
Floods, rats and volcanoes, the latter's worse:
It takes away the decency of things.

Commercial ambition's compass points
Are all identical, its virus is metastasised
Into a new algorithm which re-anoints
Old slavery: people become monetised.

There is no need to ask the question why:
It is because it is. The only doubt
Is what's the next activity to calcify,
The next business to be wiped out.

This is a wilful self-inflicted exercise,
No one's fool enough to christen it God's plan.
The reason for the dodo's swift demise?
It trusted the civility of man.

WWW

I know I'm one of one percent
who love their job and its rewards,
and age and privilege affords
me the liberty to preach dissent.

So forgive me if I shout: "I want
the internet to go away!"
even if the wine bought online today
helps to mitigate my rant.

I'm not a luddite –
luddites are romantic,
utopian and nostalgic –
but I've no idea how to fight

The solipsistic violence,
bullying, barbarism and fraud,
sites, tweets and feeds and blogposts that applaud
the pimping of pious vehemence.

Will we be forever in the clasp
of a Sisyphean endeavour
that seems to imprison whenever
freedom appears within its grasp?

And is there any plausible defence against
the drowning of the adolescent male
in a pornography Passchendaele,
choked into blind incontinence?

Let all social medias stutter
into self-induced disdain,
and like other empires drain
like sludge into the gutter.

I'm filled with suffocating gloom,
that evolution is corroded,
hope and enlightenment eroded,
and we'll go sniggering to the tomb.

Inappropriate

Inappropriate is a weasel word:
smug, prim, precious, weak,
proprietorial, half-arsed,
piss-elegant, simpering, turn-the-other-cheek,
like "making out" or "breaking wind" or "letting go"
for fuck and fart and fire

"bathrooms", "restrooms", "comfort stations"
don't hide that we all shit and piss the same
and don't gain dignity by affectation:
a lavatory is a lavatory by any name,
a friend is no less dead for having "passed away"
or insults lessened by a bureaucratic mantra

it's inadequate to use obliquity or euphemisms,
academic formulations, "ists" or "isms"
and inappropriate to say "inappropriate"
when who knows what's appropriate:
it makes you seem as if you're apologising
for your hurt or your humiliation

try scornful laughter, it wilts a rampant cock:
when propositioned on the tube or on the train
say "I'd rather grapple with a porcupine",
or flashed a penis by a wanker in the rain
say "put it away, you imbecilic swine
it's the worst of its kind I've ever seen"

challenge insults, swap genteel cowardice
for vulgar courage, call the users "bestial" or "rude"
instead of "disrespectful" and "distasteful",
try "stupid", "ignorant" "moronic", "crude",
don't try to gentrify the world or nanny it
fight back for yours and others' benefit

abusers are counting on your fear
and if you're bullied for sexual reward,
your sovereign self unrecognised,
your bruised feelings are ignored,
don't expect their lack of conscience
will poison them and lead to discontinuance

remember Simone Weil's observation:
"Love for our neighbour, is analogous to genius,
being made of creative attention;
to forget oneself briefly, identify
with a stranger to the point of fully
recognising him or her, is to defy necessity,"

force him (it's always him) to see
that you're his neighbour too
remind him that he is human:
he might know what you are due.

Soprano

Oh, Richard, your eyes are full of tears
As gutters in the rain,
Tell me what is bothering you
Why are you in such pain?

I'm crying because the sound she makes
Touches and turns my heart;
This tongue, this mouth, this throat, these lips,
Take noise, transform it into art.

Between the Notes

A mute wall halts
Niagara Falls:

The swans' flight suspended
in Sibelius' 5th

The breath as the Countess
hesitates to forgive in *Figaro*

The hush before the melody
in Beethoven's sonata No.4

Violetta's frozen thought before
renouncing her lover

The dying away at the end
of Mahler's 9th

The gap between
sound and no sound

Rests, fermatas, pauses,
caves of silence

The notes you don't play,
Miles Davis called them

When only your heartbeat
and the circulation of the blood
is audible

Notes are a sketch for sculpture,
music only when they're touched,
The rest is silence.

Pathetic Fallacy

Is it pathetic fallacy or remorse
to castigate the rain for being fierce
when rim-shots of righteous blame
force guilt to modulate to shame
and the crushing coda of a storm
insists on nothing but reform?

Embalmed in despair, lying side by side,
One swathed in fault, one carapaced in pride,
Waiting wearily for the coming of the day,
Sun rising *adagietto* can't gainsay
The need for mercy's litany to live
And the cadence: forgive, forgive, forgive.

Flight

What is it like to fly?
Look at a sparrow's labour,
Weightless, he can spurn
Lessons we must learn:
How to love our neighbour
Or what it's like to die.

Sonnet for Christopher

for Christopher Bland 1938–2017

If death is but a crossing of the world
Or a placid scull across the River Styx
With the boat's slim sails only half unfurled,
It's still a journey that no one picks
Through preference. We crowd onto the shore, keen
To honour you, to garland your farewell
With blasts of trumpets as you skim between
The banks, and winds of love and praise propel
You, friend-blessed and heart-sent, to the other side.
There you'll rest indelible in our minds' inventory
Where your wit, your open-hearted joy and pride,
Will stand with wisdom witness to your glory.
There you'll hoard the exegesis in your last breath
Of the lethal mystery of life that's death.

Face Time

Without calculation, prior intent
Or vanity, I peer into my face,
Trying to attempt – a would-be Rembrandt –
A cartographic audit of the lines that trace
The silted contours of triumph and disgrace.

I contemplate the sum of my remaining years –
A few thousand days that add up to an end
That by obvious calculation nears,
Although of course I don't intend
To accommodate it or even to pretend

My life is finite, or that my thought
Is of the rubric of the morning prayer:
That I have left undone those things I ought
To have done and done things I've been aware
Have catapulted other people to despair.

The lame mitigation persists that I try
Not to offend and I know that to accuse
Myself – "selfish" and "indulgent" might well apply –
Is just a way of offering to excuse
Myself which I, for once, stubbornly now refuse.

My facial archaeology reveals
Features stretched by age and by excess.
An aspect to the grey-green eyes conceals
Deeper feelings or forces you to guess
Whether they seek to hide or to impress.

Below them saggy pouches, sparrows-feet
And small scarred craters on the tightly
Dimpled cheeks. Is there something over-neat
And over-cautious about the brightly
White-haired goaty figure with a slightly

Rancid self-regard (or narcissism,
As they call it now)? Be your age, they say,
As if we all saw through a common prism.
But how old am I and who the hell are 'they'?
My age isn't like my shoe-size which stays

Constant, like my head, and never changes,
Unlike like my waist which has expanded
As time's passed and now ranges
From wide to wider, so I'm landed
With an alien's face and body, branded

By time, and my older self talks like a brother
To the younger like Alice to the Unicorn:
He says that now that we have seen each other,
If you'll believe in me without showing any scorn
Then I'll believe in you and both of us will warn

Each other of the necessity to act
Our age. How difficult it is in life or art
To follow the irresistible contract
Of clamour for attention and yet not depart
From modesty, its much neglected counterpart.

You have to find what's called by Diderot
"The true point", which is the line between
What you want and what you know
You shouldn't want. And I've always been
Too full of vanity and selfishness to be seen

Bothering to balance Yeats's choice:
Perfection of the work or of the life.
The first's too wearing on the second to rejoice
Or justify the pain and the remorseful strife
In paying consideration to a loving wife.

If I could find from 50 years ago
An image of my self to put beside
This one, whose faults and fears all show
Too clearly, it would demonstrate that I'd
Acquired, if not exactly wisdom, then a side

Of tenderness, of empathy, of what I'd opt
To nominate as love, an asked-for gift
That I've mishandled and have often dropped.
I now know not to waste the bounty and that if
I repay it that's a prudent sort of thrift.

The crude and true arithmetic of time
Only subtracts and doesn't ever show
Life's long division into the sublime.
Unhappily no one in death is counted as a hero
And multiples of love just figure as a zero.

Elysium

There will be nothing to replace the day
But night, not the glimmer of lights
In the café across the blue-black bay,
Nor the firefly cars flitting like bats
Down the headland road to the unseen music.

There will be no wine, no jokes, no parties,
No laughter skittering across a room,
Incendiary debates of little consequence,
Bodies conjugating with each other,
No children bearing promise in their eyes.

There will be no dawn, no birdsong,
No sun to creep over the unflecked horizon,
No sleep, no waking dreams in any colour
Of resurrection, paradise, salvation or rebirth.
There will be nothing to replace the night.

Checking Out

Shuffling towards (badge on show) Ada,
With my week's shopping, my wine and bread,
Which she blesses with her barcode reader,

She says "bag for life?" as if she divined
How much longer that might be and the thread
Of my narrative generous or malign.

Work's made me – what? – contented, doing
Something difficult that often has pleased
Others while, usually, eschewing

Schadenfreude for *Mitfreude*, its opposite,
And discovering myself as surprised
At doing it as finding there's a word for it.

I'd say I've been overfed with praise,
And been excused from poverty, immune
From struggle against gender, class or race,

Or the bad luck of exemplary parents,
Which has, of course, been my good fortune
By giving me a cause as well as torments.

Spoiled in a Ptolemaic world, I have learnt
From wife and daughter that the earth
Goes round the sun and that love is earned.

Unburdened by the baggage of the world's rebuke,
I've lived leaf-light but heavy-hearted since my birth,
And has that not been a vainglorious fluke?

What's the price in abstract nouns? Guilt? Shame?
        Doubt?
My receipt curls like a scrolled entreaty in my bag,
If it's for life, I'm not ready to check out.

The First Time

"Of course there's always a last everything"
GAVIN EWART

Of course there's always a first everything,
First masturbation, first sex, first love,
First cigarette, first drink, first drug,
First regrets, first sight of your child,
All charged with emotion because one knows;
Knowing makes them so important
And pre-empts the pretence of innocence.
A good many firsts have taken place already:
Becoming a husband, an orphan, a grandfather,
Grey hair, broken wrists and ribs, cataracts,
Night cramps, arthritis, loss of memory.
But in the catalogue of firsts one stands out alone
With no repeats, the one that I'm afraid of trying,
The ludicrously irksome first of dying.

Falling

Falling is easy and this was not the first
Accident that tore my skin and broke my bone;
My mind was sound, my feet were cursed.

Like the taste of failure, unrehearsed,
Iron in the mouth, tossed in a silent cyclone,
Falling is easy and this was not the first

Mishap or broken promise, uncoerced
By bad faith, by fear, or by being disowned:
My mind was sound, my feet were cursed.

Things valued are too easily dispersed
Love's discarded, friends outgrown;
Falling is easy and these were not the first

Blunders, slip ups, follies, grudges nursed,
With each wrong step, my guilt had been condoned:
My mind was sound, my feet were cursed.

Down, down, until the body is immersed,
I'll slip away unaccompanied, alone.
Falling is easy and this will be the first:
My mind is sound, my feet are cursed.

Funeral Music

if – sorry – when I die
you must play music
that steals my soul
like *Orfeo ed Euridice*

something to fortify
the living – don't confuse it
with a folly to extol
or even less to glorify

there'll be not a jot of me
to welcome or refuse it:
having paid death's toll
life'll trickle on indifferently

First published in Great Britain in 2018 by CHESTERMEAD

Copyright © Richard Eyre 2018

Rio: Musée de Beaux Sports was published in *Areté*; *For Tony at 80* was published in a Festschrift for Tony Harrison; *Sonnet for Christopher* was published in the *RLS* magazine.

Edited, designed and produced by Tandem Publishing
http://tandempublishing.yolasite.com/

ISBN: 978-1-5272-2720-0

10 9 8 7 6 5 4 3 2 1

A CIP catalogue record for this book is available from the British Library.

Printed and bound in Great Britain by CPI Group (UK) Ltd, Croydon CR0 4YY.